A rocke' Mo

This book belongs to

_____

Written by Stephen Barnett
Illustrated by Rosie Brooks

Contents

A rocket to the Moon 3

My new pencil 13

Staying up late 23

New words 31

What did you learn? 32

About this book

A rocket to the Moon, **A special pencil** and **Staying up late** are the stories in this book. Each one of them bringing new ideas and vocabulary to the reader.

A rocket to the Moon

It was the final countdown. . . . 5, 4, 3, 2, and then suddenly the giant rocket engine started and all I could see out of the windows were clouds of white smoke. Blast off!

Our journey to the Moon had begun. It was something I had always wanted to do.

Two months before, our teacher had told us that Space Mission was looking for a child to join their crew. They wanted just an average kind of child who could read, write and do a bit of mathematics.

This had to be me! My parents sent a letter to the school to say that it was okay for me to go to the Moon. They also said that I would do extra homework while I was away to keep up my study.

There was lots to get ready. I was measured up for my space suit. I was also taught to drive the Moon buggy which we would use when we got there.

Then there were lessons in moving about in low gravity (that was cool) and how to eat space food, which is a bit like peanut butter toothpaste. It tastes better than it sounds!

Now we were on our way. The smoke from the rocket cleared and I could see straight up into the sky. The sky was getting darker and darker as the rocket ship moved away from the earth.

Then the rocket became level and turned towards the Moon. The Moon filled the main window of the rocket, shining bright in the deep blue-black sky. I couldn't wait to be there.

It would be strange to stand on the Moon and look back to the Earth.

My new pencil

When my old drawing pencil became too small to use any more, I took my pocket money and walked with my brother to the shops to buy a new one.

The woman at the shop listened while I told her what I wanted. 'Well, I do have one special drawing pencil I found in an old box at the back of the shop,' she said. She reached under the counter and brought out a tin container. 'Here, what do you think?'

It looked like a normal kind of pencil but it was very red and very shiny. I looked at my pocket money. There was just enough to buy the pencil. I gave the money to the shopkeeper.

When I got home, I took a new sheet of white paper and sat down at the kitchen table to draw.

I was thinking that I would like to draw a picture of horses. I was thinking the horses should be brown. As I started to draw, the pencil's colour changed to brown!

Hmm. Then I thought that the colour should be a lighter shade of brown and suddenly the brown became lighter! It was just right!

I drew a white horse and then a black one. Each time I thought about which colour the horses should be, the pencil drew them in just the right shade!

I stopped drawing to have a good look at the pencil. It seemed no different from my other ones. I started again with my picture. Now I wanted to add some grass which the pencil drew in green! And a sky which changed to blue! I also drew some flowers around the edge of the field which were yellow and red!

The best thing was that the pencil never runs out.
I will have it and its magic forever!

Staying up late

When I was young I always wanted to stay up late. But my parents always said, 'Time for bed, Sharon, it's time for bed. You need your sleep.'

Why couldn't I stay up late like my older brother did? He was only a few years older than me but he got to stay up until nine o'clock. I had to go bed at eight.

Then one day, my mum said, 'Do you know, next weekend it is the end of the year. It's a special day, the last night of the year. We're going to have a party and you can stay up late if you like, even until midnight.'

Midnight! It was almost like staying up all night and never going to sleep at all!

The day of the party I helped my parents get everything ready. We cleaned the living room, prepared the food, and put up streamers and balloons. The party was to start at eight o' clock, the time when I usually went to bed.

We had lots of fun, singing and dancing. There were special foods and my brother and I were just like the grown-ups. We passed around the food and talked and sang. Then just before midnight we all gathered together, joined arms and sang a special song to welcome in the New Year.

I finally went to bed at one o'clock in the morning. I didn't get up until lunchtime and the next night for once I was happy to go to bed early!

New words

add	edge	midnight	straight
arm	field	month	streamer
average	final	older	study
balloon	gather	party	taste
black	giant	peanut butter	taught
blast	gravity	pencil	teacher
brown	grown-up	picture	think
buggy	homework	pocket money	tin
child	horse	read	toothpaste
clean	join	rocket engine	weekend
clear	journey	shade	welcome
container	keep	sharpen	white
cool	kind	shiny	write
countdown	lesson	shopkeeper	year
counter	lighter	silvery	younger
crew	living-room	sing	
dance	low	smoke	
different	lunch-time	space suit	
drawing	mathematics	special	
drive	measure	starting	

What did you learn?

A rocket to the Moon

What colour was the smoke around the rocket as it took off?

What did the boy learn to drive?

What did the boy think the space food tasted like?

My new pencil

What colour was the new pencil?

What did the boy draw?

What was the special thing about the pencil?

Staying up late

What is the name of the girl?

Why was the family having a party?

What time did the girl go to bed?